Everyday ABC's

For Toddlers

Created by Kristen Dovnik

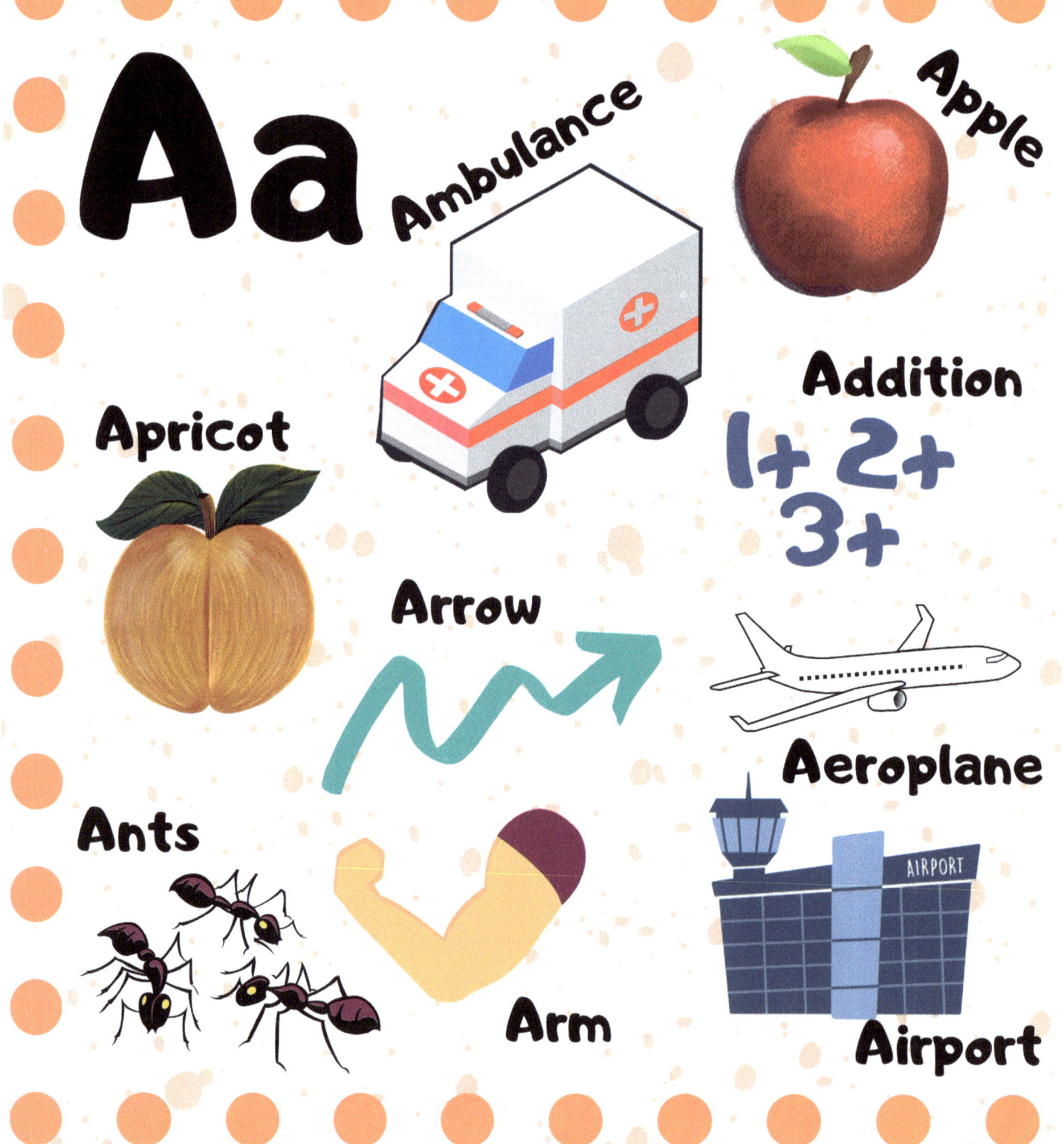

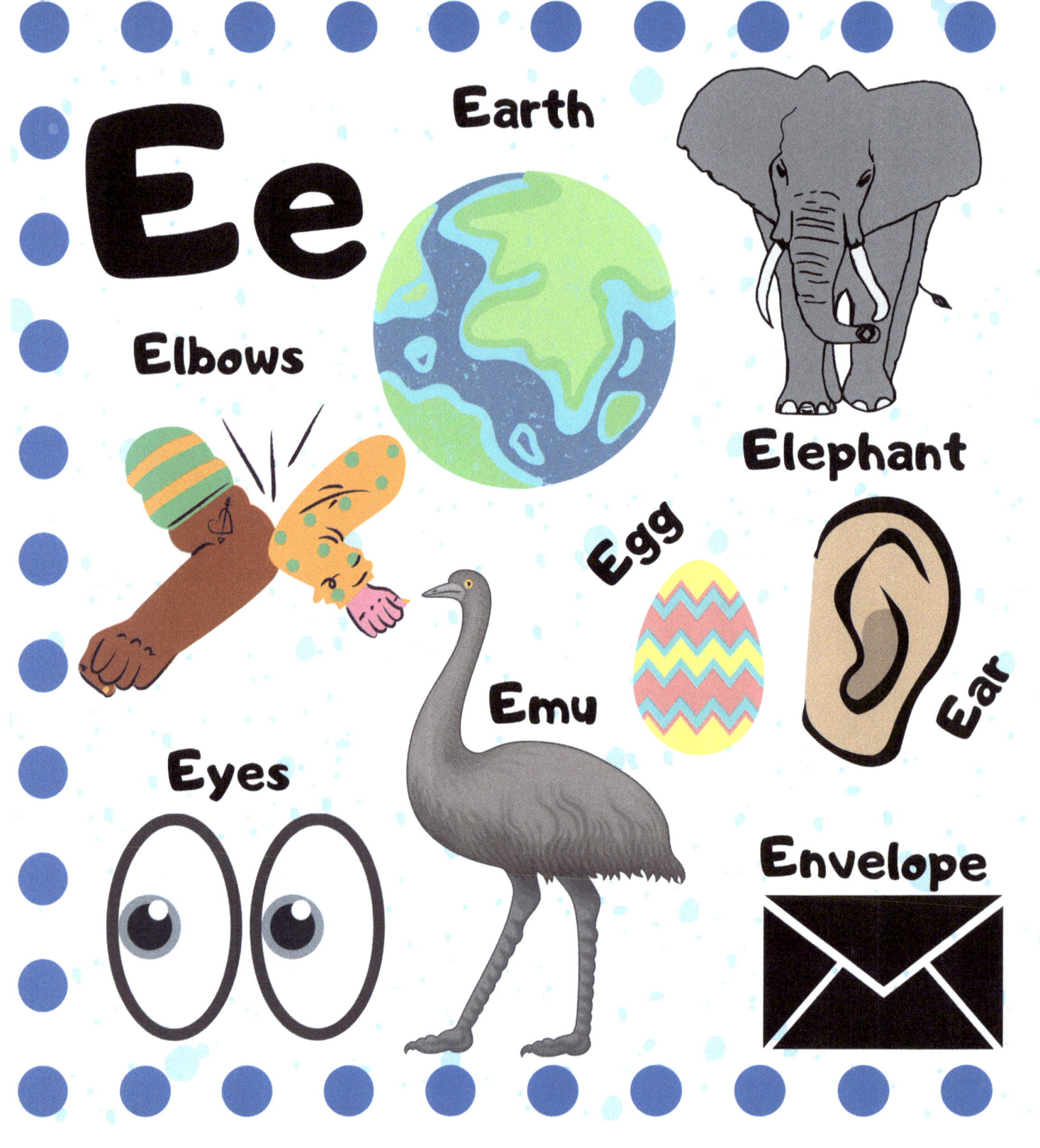

Night

Nest

Nn

Noodles

Nap

Nappy

Nose

Nuts

Necklace

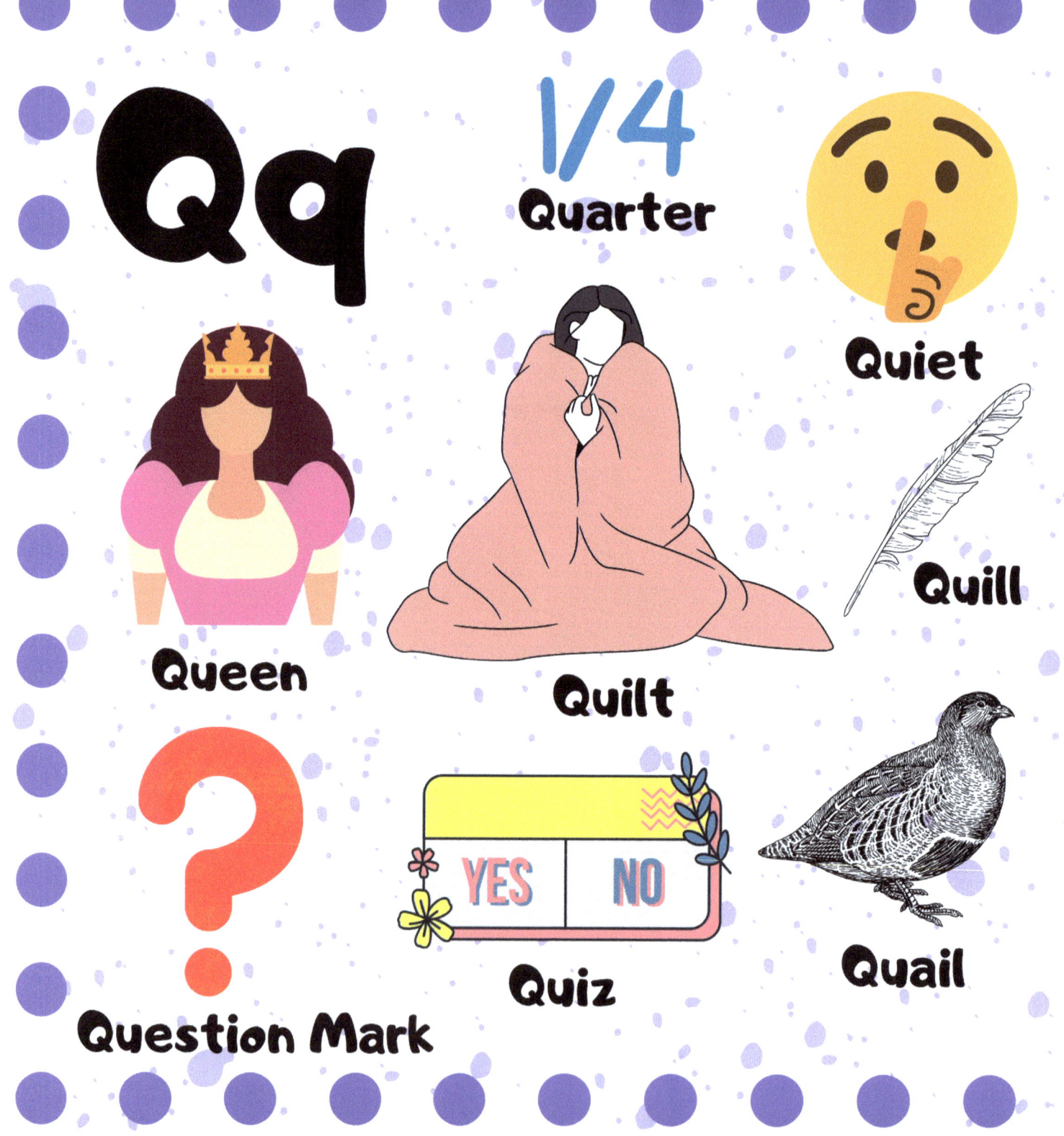

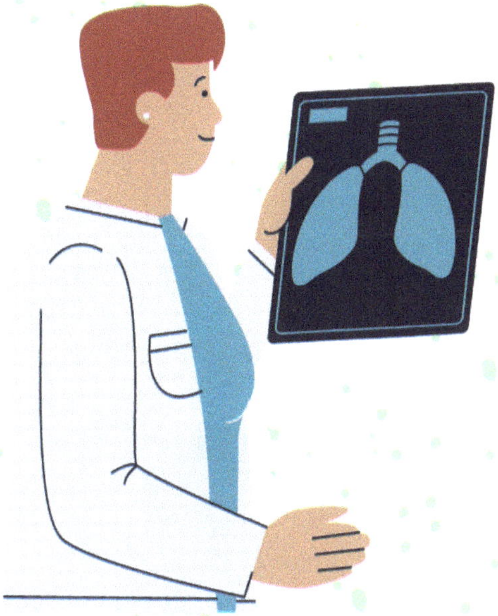

X-ray Technician

Xylophone

Xx

Xbox

Xbox Controller

X-ray

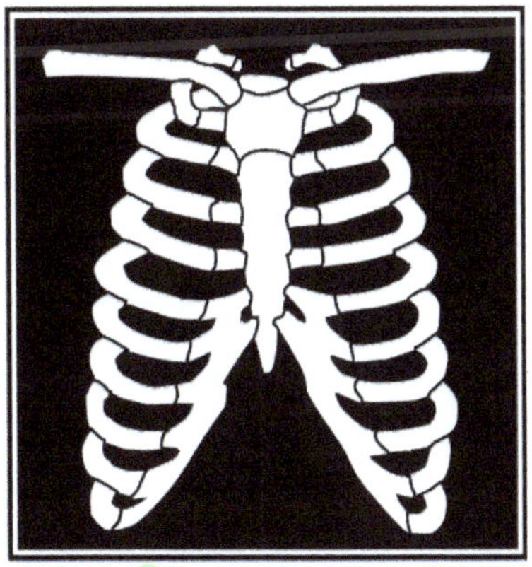

Aa Bb Cc Dd Ee
Ff Gg Hh Ii
Jj Kk Ll Mm
Nn Oo Pp Qq Rr
Ss Tt Uu Vv Ww
Xx Yy Zz

Now you know your ABC's next time won't you sing with me?

www.ingramcontent.com/pod-product-compliance
Lightning Source LLC
Chambersburg PA
CBHW061135010526
44107CB00068B/2956